PROFESSOR CAROL'S

A History of Early Sacred Music

From the Temple through the Middle Ages

ASSIGNMENTS & QUIZZES

BY CAROL B. REYNOLDS, PH.D.

Silver Age Music, Inc.
Plano, Texas

Published in the United States by Silver Age Music, Inc.
Plano, Texas

ISBN 978-0-9819990-6-7

© 2016 Silver Age Music, Inc.

All rights reserved under International and Pan-American Copyright Conventions. No part of this book may be reproduced or transmitted in any form or by any means, electronic or mechanical, including photocopying, recording, or by any information storage and retrieval system, without permission in writing from the Publisher.

Professor Carol® is a registered trademark of Silver Age Music, Inc.

Printed in the United States of America

120716

About the Assignments

The assignments for this course are intended to amplify and enrich your experience of the discussion in the video and text. We do not expect that every student will do all of the assignments, or even that *any* student will do all of them. They are presented with the expectation that students will vary significantly in age, academic level, and depth of interest in the subject.

For students pursuing the topic at a more serious level, we recommend that you read through the assignments and then spend some time considering in greater depth the topics that interest you most. You may already be proficient in some of the topics presented, and you need not do an assignment just because it's there. On the other hand, you may find it useful to reconsider some familiar topics in a new light. Or the material in a particular unit may inspire you to expand your knowledge in other directions besides those presented in the assignments.

In instances where students are approaching the subject under the guidance of a teacher or parent, we anticipate that the teacher will tailor the assignments to fit individual or class needs. The assignments in such cases should be viewed as a resource for the teacher who may use some or all of them as appropriate.

Some of the assignments are rather practical in nature, some explore the music in greater details, and others explore more philosophical issues. They are not all suited for everyone.

Essay questions are also provided within the assignments for each unit. You may choose to require and grade these essays, to treat them as an optional exercise, or to use them merely for discussion purposes.

You will find references to various websites and videos on services like YouTube. These links sometimes disappear, even though we have made a serious attempt to link only to resources that have good prospects of remaining available. We always appreciate it when students notify us of broken links or any other problems. We expect to update materials periodically at the Professor Carol website (www.professorcarol.com).

We also invite you to share your experiences on the Professor Carol Forum (forums.professorcarol.com) with others who are taking the course.

Unit 1 Assignments

Key Terms (consult the Glossary)

Chant
Credo
Gregorian chant
Liturgy
Melody
Metrical
Monastics, monks, nuns
Monody

Monophonic
Monotheism
Non-metrical
Notation
Oral transmission
Paradigm
Shema (Sh'ma)

Key Names (consult the Who's Who)

Charlemagne (Charles the Great)
St. John Chrysostom

St. John Chrysostom
Pepin

Key Places

Jerusalem

Rome

Credo

1. Read the text of the *Credo* in the Appendix of the Text.

2. The *Liber Usualis* was compiled by monks in Solesmes and contains Gregorian chants for occasions throughout the Christian Year. Consult a copy of the *Liber Usualis*. For an online or Kindle version, you can start with this link:

    https://archive.org/details/TheLiberUsualis1961

Look at the Table of Contents. Notice that after some prefatory materials, the *Liber Usualis* has a section on the Ordinary Chants of the Mass followed by a section of Ordinary Chants of the Office. "Ordinary" refers to texts that are said or sung on most every occasion. A "Mass" is a worship service that includes a celebration of the Lord's Supper. "Office" refers to the services assigned to specific hours of the day, such as Matins or Vespers. There are eight daily Offices, and for centuries many people observed them all every day. Some people still do, particularly in monasteries and convents.

Following these two sections of "ordinary chants" in the *Liber Usualis*, you find a much larger section called "The Proper of the Time." "Proper" refers to texts that change with the season of the Church Year or with specific occasions. That gives you four terms that should become quite familiar (if they are not familiar already):

- Ordinary
- Proper
- Mass
- Office

The *Credo* is part of the Ordinary of the Mass.

Turn to Chants for the Credo in your *Liber Usualis*. Look in the Table of Contents for "Ordinary Chants of the Mass: Kyrie, Gloria, &c." Chants for the Credo will be found within this category (page 64 in our version). You will see six versions of the Credo labeled Credo I, Credo II, etc.

The musical notation, or written notes, you see was developed around the year 1000 A.D. and is called "Square Notation" or "Black Notation." If you read modern notation, you will see some things that are familiar and some things that are not. We will learn more about early notation in subsequent classes. It is not necessary in this course for you to read music, modern or old. In fact, monks sang the chant for centuries before written notation was developed.

QUESTIONS ABOUT THE *LIBER USUALIS*

a. Notes are placed on lines and in spaces. How many lines do you see? How does that compare with today's musical notation?

b. What strikes you about the shapes and designs of the notes?

c. How often, and where, do you see the vertical lines on the music staff separating sections of the chant?

Guidelines for Listening

3. When studying any kind of music, the most essential element of your study should be listening to the music. Unfortunately, many people today have not developed the skill of listening well. So here are a few suggestions to guide your listening:

- Do not multitask. Put away all other activities and distractions so that you can give the music your full attention.
- Listen in a comfortable place where you will not be interrupted.

- If possible, listen using high fidelity speakers or good headphones, not on tinny earbuds.
- Listen to the same piece multiple times until you become familiar with the music. When experiencing a piece of music for the first time, it is a good practice to listen twice in immediate succession.

Of course, these suggestions apply to listening to recordings, but you should make every effort to hear the music in a live performance.

Some of these suggestions may seem obvious. Most people today, however, are bombarded constantly by music. We encounter it everywhere and most often in situations where the music is secondary to some other activity. So the idea of really doing nothing other than listening to music may be quite new to some people. If that's the case with you, you will likely find music becoming much more enjoyable and meaningful as you develop some good listening habits.

You also need to choose recordings carefully. If we were studying Beethoven, you could safely choose among many professional recordings. Some would be better performances than others, and some would have superior recording quality. We could debate the relative merits of the recordings, but all (or mostly all) would be authentic renditions of Beethoven's music. This is not true of Gregorian chant. Many recordings have been dressed up for our modern ears. Orchestral accompaniment and sound effects have been added to many performances. Admittedly, since there are some details about how chant actually sounded that we don't know for sure, there is some room for performers to get creative when they go into a studio to record Gregorian chant. There may also be good reasons for people today to use some form of accompaniment with the chant.

We are engaged, however, in an historical study, so we want to stay as close as possible to what history tells us. We know that early chant was sung without accompaniment. Later in the course we will discuss the introduction of instruments. So when you find recordings that feature organ accompaniment, or chirping birds and crashing waves, or layers of electronic sound effects, well . . . keep looking.

You may start by seeking out the handful of recordings by the Monks of St. Peter's Abbey of Solesmes (l'Abbaye Saint Pierre de Solesmes). These are available on iTunes and Amazon. We recommend them in part because you can find recordings with all of the five parts of the Ordinary of the Mass: Kyrie, Gloria, Credo, Sanctus, and Agnus Dei. These will be central to our study.

4. Listen to the *Credo*.

http://bit.ly/1xW3guR

If the link above does not work or you prefer to search on your own for other examples, keep in mind that most of the Gregorian chant you find for free on YouTube will be accompanied and, therefore, not authentic in its sound. It does not matter if you listen to Credo I or Credo II or Credo III through VI. Just get used to the sound of actual *a cappella* chant and how it expresses the text.

THINGS TO NOTICE

- The music in the *Credo* is predominantly "syllabic" – that is, one note per syllable of text. You occasionally find multiple notes on one syllable of text, specifically on the words "lúmine" and "gloria." What do those Latin words mean?

- Notice that the music moves mostly in stepwise motion (to adjacent notes) rather than in wide leaps.

- Think of ways that the "Amen" is different from the main part of the chant.

5. Compare *syllabic* and *melismatic* chant. Look at Credo I in the *Liber Usualis* (page 64). This chant is almost entirely syllabic—one note for each syllable of text. The text is rather lengthy, and chants with a lot of text tend to be syllabic. There are, however, a few places where more than one notes occurs on a single syllable of text. In the second phrase, notice the two notes (one of top of the other) on the word Pátrem. Notice also two notes that touch one another in that same phrase on the word ómnium. Where notes touch adjacent notes, this indicates more than one note on a single syllable of text. You will see several instances of this in the Credo, but for the most part the chant is syllabic.

Turn to page 25 and look for the Kyrie with the subheading "Cunctipotens Genitor Deus." The text of the Kyrie is quite short. Notice that there are many notes that occur on a single syllable of text. It is melismatic. We will refer many times in this course to syllabic and melismatic chants, so commit these terms to memory.

We will also discuss later the terms *ecstatic* and *didactic*. Look them up now in the course glossary or in your dictionary. Melismatic chant tends to be more ecstatic. Turn once more in the *Liber Usualis* to pages 95-97. You will find a series of Alleluias, all of them in a melismatic style. Why would melismatic chant be appropriate for an Alleluia?

6.   Listen to a melismatic chant sung by Mulierum Schola Gregoriana Clamaverunt Iusti, a women's ensemble in Warsaw, Poland:

> http://bit.ly/10Qacrn

The chant *Ad te domine* is an Offertory and can be found at page 321 in the *Liber Usualis*.

Essay Question

a.   In either your own congregation, or another church or synagogue you might visit, what role does "chanting" play in the worship service? If there is chanting, what texts are chanted? Is the chanting led by a single person (cantor) or a small or large choir? Do the members of the congregation participate and, if so, to what degree?

b.   If you were able to suggest that some spoken texts be changed to chant, which would you choose? Biblical passages? Prayers? Responses? What would be your reason(s) for selecting these passages?

10 Early Sacred Music – Assignments & Quizzes

Unit 2 Assignments

Key Terms (consult the Glossary)

Antiphonal
Archeology
Ark of the Covenant
Babylonian exile
Cantillation
Diaspora
First Temple
Hallel
Holy of Holies

Levites
Mishna
Pastoral
Precentor
Sacrifice
Second Temple
Synagogue
Talmud
Torah

Key Names (consult the Who's Who)

Cyrus the Great
Herod the Great
Miriam
King Solomon

King
Isaiah
Nebuchadnezzar

Key Places

Babylon
Dome of the Rock
Jerusalem
Mount Moriah
Robinson's Arch

City of David
Holy Sepulcher
Masada
Mount of Olives
Tyre

The Temple

1. Here is a timeline of the major events surrounding the Temple. Please know there is much disagreement about dates.

BC (B.C.E)

c. 1200	Israelites settle in Canaan.
c. 1020	Saul anointed first king of Israel.
c. 1000	The Jebusite stronghold of Jerusalem is captured by King David.
c. 1000-970	King David rules over Israel.
c. 962/65	Solomon builds the First Temple.
c. 910-925	First Temple plundered by Egyptians (there will be other

	instances of sacking, plundering, destruction, followed by repairs).
599-97	Babylonian Period. First Babylonian Siege under Nebuchadnezzar; First group of Jews carried of into captivity.
587-86	Final destruction of First Temple by Babylonians/Nebuchadnezzar. Murder, plunder, and the end of Jerusalem. Many taken into captivity.
539/38	King Cyrus captures Babylon.
538	Edict of Cyrus allows Jews to return home.
c. 516	Rebuilding of the Temple (first version of Second Temple) under Darius the Great. (There will be many more disruptions and plundering and problems for the next centuries.)
332	Alexander the Great conquers Jerusalem
167	Maccabean Revolt
63	Roman Empire controls the Land of Israel.
19-6	Herod expands and refurbishes Second Temple.
A.D. (C.E.)	Birth of Christ
63	Jerusalem captured by Roman General Pompey. Period of Jewish-Roman warring.
70	Siege of Jerusalem. Titus captures and destroys the Second Temple, Jerusalem.
132-135	Bar Kokhba Revolt
136	Hadrian expels Christians and Jews from Jerusalem
210	Mishna edited by Rabbi Yehudah ha-Nasi.

2. Visiting the Second Temple

Computer graphics have made possible excellent "virtual tours" of the Second Temple, including the two listed below. Each has advantages, and the second will provide much specific information about what you're seeing.

Before you start watching either clip, write down a few ideas/speculations you may have about what the temple must have been like: how it must have felt to walk into it, observe (or prepare) the sacrifices, and hear the cantillated texts and blessings.

    http://bit.ly/15B8iW2

    http://bit.ly/1CI0QVW

QUESTIONS

    a.   Having seen one or more "virtual tours," which did you find most helpful? Why?

    b.   Has seeing them changed your initial speculations?

    c.   What in particular did the 3-D graphics add to your understanding?

    d.   Is there anything you would add or change if you were the one creating such a 3-D "tour"?

Cantillation

3.   Masoretic Signs, Tropes, and Introduction to Cantillation of the Torah

For this part of the assignment, it does not matter that you (likely) do not read Hebrew. The video by Cantor Michael Weis will open doors to understanding how Torah and other texts are notated and, in particular, learned by modern students today. Don't worry about what you don't know (the Hebrew alphabet, the meaning of the Hebrew words).

Instead, look at how Cantor Weis is teaching how to approach mastering the tropes (signs indicating the musical patterns) and explaining the best way to go about becoming comfortable with the process.

Also, if it is new to you, how do you find yourself responding to reading "right to left"? If you already know Hebrew or a similar language, of course, you do this regularly.

    http://bit.ly/1tefBxE

Points in the Weis Video

By the time you get to minute 6:00 or so, Cantor Weis will have laid the groundwork and you'll be into his method of teaching, visually and aurally.

By minute 9:00 or so, you'll see how he lays out a clever symbol system for "pick-ups."

Cantor Weis has many excellent videos. You can click to find them on YouTube. Specifically, if you'd like to see how more about how he teaches students techniques for mastering Torah readings—as well as his work method and practice tips—then you may enjoy this video as well (c. 20 minutes). The discipline and exactness he proposes can be applied to many things.

The Psalms

4. Do you have a favorite Psalm? If so, which one, and why?

Thinking about it, are you at all aware of its structure? (the division of the lines, repeated lines)

Look at its text. What do you find? Are the lines divisible in halves? Are there short lines also? Do you see any patterns in line repetition?

After you've analyzed your favorite Psalm this way, does your new understanding of the structure change or add to anything you have liked about the Psalm?

5. The Hallel

Highly important is the cantillation of a group of Psalms known as the Hallel. The Hallel covers Psalms 113 to 118, which is a lot of text! The Hallel covers many aspects of Jewish history, including the Exodus from Egypt, the splitting of the Red Sea, the giving of the Torah, the revival of the dead, and the difficulties preceding the Messianic Age. And, in case you're wondering, the word Hallelujah is related to Hallel.

A. Here is the opening of one of the Psalms in the Hallel: Psalm 114 from the Hebrew Bible.

http://bit.ly/1BbSMZf

Click at the top and listen to it in Hebrew. You should be able to follow by listening for familiar words" Yisrael, Jakob, Jordon, Adon[ai] (Lord), Elohin (God)

Track how each verse falls into two sections. Listen for the spacing.

Think about how singers might handle these two sections. Solo singing for the first half? Choral response for the second? Two choruses back and forth? Etc.

B. Visit www.myjewishlearning.com and type "Hallel" in the search box. Read the explanation of the Hallel. You will read that it is chanted on all major festivals except Rosh-ha-Shanah and The Day of Atonement.

QUESTIONS

    a.   What is Rosh-ha-Shanah?

    b.   What is The Day of Atonement? Does it have another name one popularly hears?

    c.   You will read that there is a difference of opinion among the early authorities as to whether the obligation to recite the Hallel is biblical or rabbinical. What does that mean (to you)?

6. Review the various types of evidence that help us understand music-making in Old Testament times. How can each of these add something to our understanding?

- Archeological evidence. The study of human activity in the past primarily through material objects and environmental data.
- Philological evidence – *philos* (love of) + *logos* (word or reason). A love of learning, of literature as well as of argument and reasoning.
- Morphological evidence. The study of form and structure.
- Oral tradition. The passing of knowledge verbally from one generation to another.
- Biblical accounts

Essay Question

a. In what ways has learning about the history of worship in the Temple helped you better understand the worship in your own denomination? Describe some of the most important similarities? What are the biggest differences?

b. Does learning about worship in the Temple help you better understand worship in denominations other than your own?

16 Early Sacred Music – Assignments & Quizzes

Unit 3 Assignments

Key Terms (consult the Glossary)

Acoustics
Aerophone
Aulos
Chordophone
Hellenistic
Homophonic
Idiophone

Kithara
Lyre
Membranophone
Musica humana
Musica instrumentalis
Musica mundane
Rhetoric

Key Names (consult the Who's Who)

Alexander the Great
Pythagoras

Plato

Key Places

Athens
Rome
Villa San Marco, Castellammare di Stabia

Mount Vesuvius
Theater of Dionysus

Music of the Spheres

1. "Music of the Spheres" is a term that has continued to appeal across the centuries. As one example, a musical organization in New York that has adopted the name produces concerts and lectures that "illuminate music's historical, philosophical and scientific foundations."

QUESTIONS

    a. What do you think a common response among your friends might be to the phrase "Music of the Spheres"?

    b. What other uses in popular culture does "Music of the Spheres" have today?

Consider Boethius's three-fold division of music. *See* Text p. 40. Think of some modern-day examples that would fit into these categories:

- *Musica mundana* (or Music of the Spheres)
- *Musica humana*

- *Musica instrumentalis*

2. Pythagoras and Music Theory

Look up the difference between Pythagorean tuning and the equal-temperament tuning system used today for fixed pitch instruments.

Fixed pitch instruments are those that do not allow the instrumentalist to make fine adjustments to the frequency of the pitch. The piano is an excellent example. A pianist can control many aspects of the sound: articulation, volume, some aspects of timbre. But not the pitch frequency. In contrast, players of wind instruments can make fine adjustments in the tuning of each note as they play, and players of string instruments with unfretted fingerboards (like the violin) have the full continuum of frequencies available to them. The same is true for singers.

What difference does this make? We answer that question by noting that all music is based on mathematical relationships. The tonal system that we use in the West has a foundation in mathematical and physical properties. But our tonal system also comes into conflict with aspects of physics.

3. Tuning Systems

Looking at math and acoustics in detail may leave you utterly fascinated or completely bored, but John Crooks presents it in a way that is likely to be accessible to many in his video series "Introduction to Pitch Systems in Tonal Music." You can watch the full series of videos at this link.

http://bit.ly/21K3wxm

You can also access the series at http://ocw.uci.edu/lectures (select the category "art").

You can watch the whole series or focus in on video 5 and video 6 that deal more specifically with Pythagorean tuning.

Does seeing the frequencies and waveforms on an oscilloscope help you hear the fine distinctions in tuning?

Music and Morality

4. "Music is a moral law. It gives soul to the universe, wings to the mind, flight to the imagination, and charm and gaiety to life and to everything." – Plato

Plato wrote about music in this passage from the *The Republic*:

> We said we did not require dirges and lamentations in words.
>
> We do not.
>
> What, then, are the dirge-like modes of music? Tell me, for you are a musician.
>
> The mixed Lydian, he said, and the tense or higher Lydian, and similar modes.
>
> These, then, said I, we must do away with. But again, drunkenness is a thing most unbefitting guardians, and so is softness and sloth.
>
> Yes.
>
> What, then, are the soft and convivial modes?
>
> There are certain Ionian and also Lydian modes that are called lax. Will you make any use of them for warriors?
>
> None at all, he said, but it would seem that you have left the Dorian and the Phrygian.
>
> I don't know the musical modes, I said, but leave us the mode that would fittingly imitate the utterances and the accents of a brave man who is engaged in warfare or in any enforced business, and who, when he has failed, either meeting wounds or death or having fallen into some other mishap, in all these conditions confronts fortune with steadfast endurance and repels her strokes. And another for such a man engaged in works of peace, not enforced but voluntary, either trying to persuade somebody of something and imploring him - whether it be a god, through prayer, or a man, by teaching and admonition - or contrariwise yielding himself to another who is petitioning him or teaching him or trying to change his opinions, and in consequence faring according to his wish, and not bearing himself arrogantly, but in all this acting modestly and moderately and acquiescing in the outcome. Leave us these two modes - the enforced and the voluntary - that will best imitate the utterances of men failing or succeeding, the temperate, the brave - leave us these.
>
> Well, said he, you are asking me to leave none other than those I just spoke of.

The Republic 398d-399c.

QUESTIONS

    a.   Do Plato's opinions surprise you? Are there points on which you strongly agree or disagree?

    b.   Can you imagine having a similar serious conversation with someone today about aspects of music? If so, what issues might it address?

5.   Read this article, "Music and Morality," by contemporary philosopher Roger Scruton. Again, you may find points on which you strongly agree or disagree.

    http://spectator.org/articles/40193/music-and-morality

QUESTIONS

    a.   Does Scruton strike you as just an old guy who doesn't understand the music of contemporary youth culture? If not, how would you describe his standpoint?

    b.   Do you understand his distinction between (a) rhythm that organizes sound into movement and (b) computer-generated rhythm that simply slices time into repeatable units? What element is missing from the latter? Can you hear the difference?

    c.   Does he persuade you that Plato was asking very similar questions and that the issues today are very similar to the issues in ancient times?

    d.   Do you believe that there is a moral quality in music entirely separate from any text that may be associated with it? Does your answer to this question affect your view of what music is appropriate for sacred worship?

Essay Question

How would you describe to someone what you now understand about music in the early centuries of Christian worship in Rome? What aspects do we know from historical evidence? What aspects are based more on traditions that have come down to us?

Unit 4 Assignments

Key Terms (consult the Glossary)

Aniconic
Apostolic
Augustus
Caesar
Catacombs
Catechumen
Chi Rho
Edict

Feast
Fresco
Mosaic
Pagan
Patristic
Pax Romana
Sepulcher
Tetrarchy

Key Names (consult the Who's Who)

Caesar Augustus
Constantius
Galerius
Josephus
Maxentius
St. Cecilia
Theodosius

Constantine
Diocletian
Hadrian
Julius Caesar
Maximian
St. Helena
Titus

Key Places

Acropolis
Constantinople
Gaul
Jerusalem
Milvian Bridge
Phoenicia
Rubicon

Assyria
Eastern Empire
Hippo
Mars Hill
Nicaea
Rome
Western Empire

Oxyrhynchus Hymn

1. The Oxyrhynchus Hymn (P.Oxy. XXX 2507) was discovered in 1918. It is the oldest known notation of early Christian music. You can learn about the multi-spectral imaging process behind this discovery at POxy: Oxyrhynchus Online, found at this link:

   http://www.papyrology.ox.ac.uk/POxy/

You may be interested in reading about the ancient city of Oxyrhynchus. If you are particularly interested in the papyri and want to know how scholars work, the interviews done by the Hellenic Society will provide much more detail.

> http://bit.ly/1RsfnsG

Roman Empire Timeline

2. Review some of the major events in Roman history with this timeline and see how Rome expanded its territory to include all of the Mediterranean and subsequently lost the Western Empire.

> http://bit.ly/1L9xHqo

QUESTIONS

> a. What reasons can you cite for why Rome was able to conquer so much territory?
>
> b. The factors that contribute to Rome's eventual demise are many, and people may have different views on the primary causes and the significance of some of the historical events. Can you find two or three factors that most people agree were major contributors to Rome's fall?

Languages

3. We were very fortunate to spend some time recently with historian Dr. Jacques Pauwels. Actually, Professor Carol and Dr. Pauwels were both speakers on ship making a transatlantic crossing. We so enjoyed his presentations. People in his audience with no previous interest in the ancient world expressed their delight at the way he made ancient history interesting. Dr. Pauwels graciously agreed to talk on camera about the languages of the Middle East in ancient times. On the busy ship, we were not able to find a good location to film this discussion. After all, when you're in the middle of the Atlantic, with the bottom 14,000 feet below, you can't be too picky. But Dr. Pauwels clarifies many important aspects of this history, and his talk is well worth watching in its entirety.

> https://vimeo.com/157622700

Unit 4 / Page 23

QUESTIONS

a. Language is a fundamental element of culture. How does Dr. Pauwels' explanation of which languages were used at certain times in the ancient world (and why they became prominent) help you understand the history better? Give two or three examples, if you can.

b. Think about the power and influence of English in the world today. What might be said 500 years from now about the role of English in global culture?

c. See what you can find online concerning efforts by France to keep English terms from coming into common usage. Why do you think France has done this? Is it a reasonable thing for France to do?

d. Look up the history of the Hebrew language. Dr. Pauwels explains that in Jesus' time it had become a liturgical language rather than one in everyday usage. How do you think a language reaches the point where it is used only for religious purposes?

e. Why did the people of Israel today bring back Hebrew as the official language of their country? Was there any significant opposition to doing that? Why do you think some people might oppose that?

f. Are you surprised that Latin was not in wider use throughout the Roman Empire in the 1st Century AD? Visit the site below concerning the History of the Latin language.

http://bit.ly/1LbPsWc

Architecture

4. The following video contains architectural animations of the Church of the Holy Sepulcher going back in time.

http://bit.ly/1RqO8Ok

You may find this helpful in comprehending the confusing structure of this important site and the various modifications it has experienced over time. For an in-depth description of the site and its archeology, you may refer to this article by Tom Powers:

> http://bit.ly/1OXf4el

5. Read this paper by Kim Williams on "Symmetry in Architecture."

> http://bit.ly/1OX1k39

You may want to refer back to this article later in the course when we study Gothic Architecture.

QUESTIONS

- a. How does the Christian architecture of Constantine's time reflect Christian understanding?

- b. Examine the architecture of your own church or of another church that you can physically visit.
    - (1) What types of symmetry can you find in this church?
    - (2) In what ways is this church similar or different to the architecture of Constantine's time?
    - (3) How, and on what, does the architecture of this church focus the worshipper?

- c. Do you think the architects of Constantine's time considered the question of music and acoustics within the church?

Essay Question

The video for this unit contains recreations of Ancient Roman music by Synaulia. You've had a chance to hear certain aspects of their recreations of this Roman music, including (a) melodies, (b) rhythms, (c) playing of instruments, (d) costumes, and (e) choreography (dance). What would be the challenges of recreating these elements? What aspects would seem to be most historically accurate? Which would be least likely to be accurate? What are some of the archeological resources and documents they have used to recreate these things?

Unit 5 Assignments

Key Terms (consult the Glossary)

Abbot
Ascetic
Benedictine
Compline
Lauds
Matins
Monastery
Monk
None

Office
Peregrinus
Prime
Rorate caeli
Sext
Terce
Vespers
Vigil

Key Names (consult the Who's Who)

St. Anthony the Great
St. Augustine
St. John Cassian
Franz Liszt

St. Athanasius
St. Benedict
St. John Chrysostom
St. Pachomius

Key Places

Ampleforth Abbey
Egypt
St. Louis Abbey

Clear Creek Monastery
Monte Cassino

Monasticism

1. Depending on your own religious background, you may be familiar with the basic information and the images you'll see in these videos. But if you're not, it is useful to understand the concept of vocation. The call to a religious life (*vocare*) is built upon many things. Something as important as the cycle of celebrating the Daily Offices makes far more "sense" when the overall shape of daily religious life is understood. Understanding more of the structure and life of monastics allows us to see how the Offices are not "interruptions" to the day, but provide the basic momentum of the day.

    A. In this video by the Dominican Fathers of the Western Province of the Preachers of Jesus, you will hear the monks express their thoughts on the Liturgy of the Hours (Daily Offices).

        http://bit.ly/1DbBrC7

26 Early Sacred Music – Assignments & Quizzes

This clip contains music sung by the "Frozen Friars" in Alaska (www.frozenfriars.com)--in case you think monks don't have a sense of humor.

  B. This video will reinforce many of the concepts in this unit. You'll hear an explanation of each Daily Office and what it is like to live in that cycle of prayer from Fr. Jeremy Driscoll, OSB from Mount Angel Abbey in St. Benedict, Oregon.

  http://bit.ly/18luAga

POINTS TO NOTE FROM THIS VIDEO

- There is a strong emphasis on the term Opus Dei.

- You will follow the cycle of a monk's day, starting with Vigil.

- The times shown will show a schedule with the adjustments one often finds, where Vigil, Lauds, etc., are clustered together.

- Virtually everything you will hear is sung in English.

- This excerpt helps make clear the critical point that "Mass/Eucharist" is celebrated daily, but it is not part of the Offices. It stands outside of and independent of the Offices.

  C. Lest you think monastics are all men, here's a very useful documentary that provides a peek into the life of monastic women.

It will help emphasize the point that monasticism—structure, aesthetic, and the principles that bind it together—is similar, no matter where or when. So, meet some Carmelite Nuns from . . . India. They live in the Yercaud Carmel Community. And you'll get a look at traditional tasks, including candle-making, stitching of vestments, and the way that the Communion Host (bread) is baked, at least in this place, in the Western tradition of unleavened bread.

  http://bit.ly/1CsRlto

Monte Cassino

2. In the video for this unit, you see a photo of Monte Cassino high on a mountain not far from Rome. St. Benedict established this monastery in about 529 and lived there until his death. It was here that he wrote his Rule. Keep in

mind that the monastery has seen centuries of growth and change in architectural style.

Read the history of Monte Cassino in the Catholic Encyclopedia, a reference work completed in 1914. Missing from this particular history, of course, is the subsequent history of World War II. If you search today for information on Monte Cassino, you will find far more references to the Battle of Monte Cassino than to the work of the monastery. The monastery was destroyed by Allied forces advancing on Rome in 1944.

Bundesarchiv, Bild 146-2005-0004 / Wittke / CC-BY-SA

The Abbey has since been restored.

> http://bit.ly/1CsROfd

Visit the Monte Cassino web site.

> http://bit.ly/1OTV5pU

The Rule of St. Benedict

3. The Order of St. Benedict has its own website where you can find a wealth of materials covering Benedictine history, monastic life, spiritual reading, historical documents, and current events. The Rule of St. Benedict is reproduced there in full:

> http://bit.ly/1sYEQFB

For more on the Rule of St. Benedict, read the commentary and answer the questions at this web site:

    http://bit.ly/1TmDpGV

Our Lady of Clear Creek Abbey

4.   We visited Our Lady of Clear Creek Abbey in Oklahoma during the filming of this course, and we feature some music recorded by the monks there. Abbot Philip Anderson was interviewed on EWTN about the monastic life and the establishment of this monastery.

    http://bit.ly/1VbR5t0

Essay Question

a.   Why were the monasteries critical to the preservation of knowledge during the Middle Ages? What features of monastic life gave them this ability or, to ask another way, what made the monks good candidates to undertake this important task?

b.   Can you identify other people or institutions in Europe at the time that might have accomplished essentially the same thing? Explain.

c.   What aspects of monastic life are most different from the life we lead in modern times? How were, and are, their lives entwined with music in ways quite different from ours?

Unit 6 Assignments

Key Terms (consult the Glossary)

Mass
Ordinary
Proper
Kyrie
Gloria
Credo
Sanctus
Benedictus
Agnus Dei
Scroll

Papyrus
Parchment
Codex
Quire
Palaeography
Line Fillers
Stichometric Notes
Nomina sacra
Scriptio continua

Key Places

Cluny

Liturgical Year and Colors

1. Each part of the Church year has a color associated with it. These colors vary slightly from one Christian tradition to another, but they are by and large uniform in the Western traditions. Look at how the colors signify the various events in the Christian year and try to determine whether and how your or a friend's religious denomination uses the colors.

    http://bit.ly/1yO8JRn

The Mass

2. The full text of the Ordinary of the Mass appears in the Appendix at the back of the Text. Take time to become familiar with the parts of the Mass Ordinary and the text.

3. As you listen to the Kyrie in the video for this unit, follow along if you can at page 25 in the *Liber Usualis*. Follow the excerpt of the Gloria sung by Dr. Dodds at page 26.

The Abbey at Cluny

4. Read more about the Abbey at Cluny:

    http://bit.ly/1Pfx8QZ

Visiting Cluny today, one finds a modern visitor's center, beautiful landscaping, carefully preserved "ruins," and digital recreations. All of these things help reconstruct the grandeur and tragedy of Cluny. In answering the two questions below, feel free to consult any resources you wish, including articles, encyclopedias, and websites.

QUESTIONS

      a.   If you were to take someone through Cluny today, what points would be most important to explain about its foundation, mission, achievements, and destruction? What would be one or two facts about Cluny that you think would be most impressive to someone new to the topic?

      b.   Are there aspects of Cluny that strike you as "modern"? If so, identify a few of them, and make comparisons where you can to the modern world. Think in terms of religious, charitable, and academic institutions as well as commercial and tourist businesses.

      c.   Research more about the tragic end of Cluny and the closing and destruction of monasteries and churches in the wake of the French Revolution. Can you draw any comparisons between this epoch of history and events in today's world?

The Codex

5.   Read this article from the *New York Times* on the change from scroll to codex and consider the author's argument that we are now experiencing a similar shift with digital media.

      http://nyti.ms/1JR7BFb

6.   Spend time getting acquainted with this single historically important codex (manuscript book) containing the writings of St. Paul.

      http://bit.ly/1DbQZWx

The focus is on gathering useful vocabulary as well as considering the issues that surround "old" written materials (of which we will be encountering more and more). Think about layout and the skills needed to deal with such documents.

7.   Read/click through/explore each page of the material which explains the format, history, and writing of the document.

http://www.lib.umich.edu/reading/Paul/

Begin by focusing on the physical format of the codex, including learning about the quire. Look for the following vocabulary words as you go through the website's pages.

- Vocabulary
- Scroll
- Papyrus
- Parchment
- Codex
- Codices
- Quire
- Single-quire
- Papyrologist
- Archeological context
- Palaeography (Paleography)

Now spend time looking at the codex (digitally): discovering how the pages are formulated, what is actually written on the pages, and how to interpret it.

- Greek Page Numbers
- Paragraphos
- Line Fillers
- Titles (practices within codices)
- Stichometric Notes
- Nomina sacra
- Scriptio continua

8. Actual Reading of the Document

You can follow all of the rubrics through, and learn even more about the handwriting, abbreviations, and other details. And you can practice reading / transliterating the Greek whether or not you know any Greek. Enjoy how thorough and helpful the tools are on this part of the site. You can highlight the text for extra clarity; bring up a pop-up Greek alphabet shown in the scribe's own usage (!), and click through to a letter-by-letter transliteration to see how well you're doing! All of the lines are there, but you can jump anywhere to experience the process, such as here.

http://bit.ly/15DUx8B

Essay Question

a.   As you have learned, it's important to understand that the Mass combines the recurring (permanent) texts of the Ordinary with texts of the Proper that change for specific seasons of the liturgical year. What effect do you believe this combination had on worshippers back in the Middle Ages? What about today?

b.   Describe some features within your own worship tradition that stay the same at each service. Then describes some features that change with the occasion. What role does music play in each of these situations?

Unit 7 Assignments

Key Terms (consult the Glossary)

Anglo-Saxon
Anno domini
Antiphon
Barbarian
Black notation
Carolingian
Dark Ages

Heighted nuumes
Liber Usualis
Merovingian
Miniscule
Neume
Vespers

Key Names (consult the Who's Who)

Alcuin
Charles Martel
Clovis I
Henry II
Huns
Pepin the Short
St. Augustine of Canterbury
Thomas Becket
Visigoths

Bede
Charles the Great
Goths
Henry VIII
Mohammed
Pope Gregory
St. Boniface
Vandals

Key Places

Aachen
Britain
Canterbury
Danube River
Germany
Kent
Poitiers
Rhine-Main-Danube Canal
Sicily
York

Arabia
Byzantium
Constantinople
Gaul
Italy
Northumbria
Rhine River
Rome
Western Roman Empire

Carolingian Miniscule

1. For a brief history of Carolingian Miniscule, review this site.

    http://bit.ly/1EMRFTi

The web site Scribescribbling has an interesting article on Carolingian Miniscule and numerous other materials on calligraphy, inks, and scripts.

> http://bit.ly/1EMSGuR

Reading some of these materials will give you a sense of the skill and craftsmanship that goes into this art and, hopefully, a better appreciation for the beauty of Medieval manuscripts.

This video provides an overview of the achievements of the Carolingian Renaissance.

> http://bit.ly/1H1zNZR

Neumes

2. You may want to look at more of this 10th-century neume (neumatic) notation here.

> http://bit.ly/1y0qAaJ

Then, compare the manuscript with this later one from the 12th century.

> http://bit.ly/1H1G2Nq

The neumes in the later manuscript appear on a 4-line staff. You can see the red line clearly, which denotes F. (Notice the clef designation "f" at the beginning of each line.) It may be more difficult to see the other 3 lines of the staff, which are "incised" but not inked.

3. In the following example, you hear the chant *Orbita solaris* sung from the 12th-century neumatic notation.

> http://bit.ly/1z3scDp

Canadian musicologist James Grier has identified a monk at St. Martial in Limoges as likely responsible for this innovation: Adémar de Chabannes (c. 989-1034). He identified Adémar's handwriting and was able to show that Adémar had written all of the music notation in two manuscripts from a monastery in Aquitaine called St. Martial, one of the most important musical centers of the era.

> http://www.professorcarol.com/latest-heighted-neumes/

Canterbury

4.   The history of Canterbury is critical to the religious history of England, and it is virtually impossible to take up the topic of Canterbury without discussing St. Thomas Becket. Although Becket is somewhat removed from the time under discussion in this unit, Canterbury will continue to be a part of the discussion and you may want to explore that history now. There are many documentaries on Becket, the history of Canterbury Cathedral, the rebuilding of the Cathedral after it burned shortly after Becket's murder, and its destruction during Henry VIII's reign. And, of course, there is the full-length 1964 movie "Becket" with Richard Burton and Peter O'Toole.

Read more about the history of Canterbury Cathedral on the Sacred Destinations web site:

> http://bit.ly/1VbR5t0

We will study Gothic cathedral architecture in greater detail in Unit 11.

Essay Question

a.   Charlemagne put a high value on standardizing everything he could across his vast Holy Roman Empire. What benefits do you believe Charlemagne, and people within his realm, might realize from the standardization of education, liturgy, and music?

b.   Can you think of other times in history when rulers have sought to standardize diverse aspects of life in their kingdoms?

36 Early Sacred Music – Assignments & Quizzes

Unit 8 Assignments

Key Terms (consult the Glossary)

Cantus firmus
Codex
Consonant
Contrary motion
Diabulus in musica
Dissonant
Folio
Gathering
Guidonian hand
Hexachord
Illumination
Lombard
Manuscript

Marginalia
Miniature
Neumes
Oblique motion
Organum
Papyrus
Parallel motion
Parchment
Polyphony
Provenance
Scribe
Scriptorium

Key Names (consult the Who's Who)

Charlemagne
Léonin
Pérotin

Guido of Arezzo
Paul the Deacon

Key Places

Aachen
Monte Cassino

Lombardy
Notre Dame de Paris

Illuminations

1. In this unit's assignment, you will be asked to watch and consider several videos that convey much information about manuscripts.

This first video by Dr. Sally Dormer at Gresham College provides, in a little more than an hour, considerable details about the making of illuminated manuscripts It is well worth your time.

> http://bit.ly/15EcjZf

How To Study a Manuscript

2. The following videos provide a very detailed look at a 15th-Century manuscript. While this is from a time later than our current focus in this course,

nevertheless we think you will find it interesting and instructive to see the manuscript up close and to see the meticulous detail that scholars apply to such a resource. The videos are very well produced and explained by early music historian Hendrik Vanden Abeele who performs with the vocal group Psallentes. Don't worry about the details. The point of this exercise is merely to see the manuscript and how the manuscript might be studied. The extended series of videos will go through *all* 600 pages of the manuscript one page at a time. Consequently, we have selected three of the videos.

> http://bit.ly/1Dcd5s3

The first video (the introduction) will show you the cover and provide a few basic details. A few terms and background facts may help your understanding. The manuscript is a 1481 Antiphonary (a collection of antiphons and chants sung at Mass and the Daily Offices) from the Abbey of St. Bavo in Ghent. You will hear references to "folios," "verso" (left), and "recto" (right). A brief explanation of these terms can be found here.

> https://en.wikipedia.org/wiki/Folio

Now watch Episode 1:

> http://bit.ly/1H1PiRr

We now jump to Episode 63 dealing with the verso of Folio 30 and the recto of Folio 31. "Quire" refers to a "gathering" of folded sheets of parchment, or as Abeele says, "a bundle of folios."

> http://bit.ly/1Slr7lx

These pages contain Responsories for the Office of Matins. Abeele compares this page to a 12th-century Antiphonary to show that the melody and text has remained virtually the same for 300 years. The 12th-Century manuscript from Klosterneuburg is written in older notation using neumes on a staff. The single red line shows the F clef, with other lines of the staff marked with a dry point (no ink). If you stop the video on the Klosterneuburg manuscript, you may see the very faint dry-point lines of the staff above and below the red line for F (best visible at the bottom left).

Now if you would like to watch all 600 videos, that would be a very interesting and instructive thing to do. But we are not assigning it as part of this course.

The Medieval Manuscript Manual

3.   This Medieval Manuscript Manual was created in the course of various cultural heritage-projects at the Department of Medieval Studies at Central European University, Budapest. It provides basic information on the topic of Medieval Manuscripts for non-specialists in the field, deals with many aspects of bookmaking, and contains numerous illustrations.

    http://bit.ly/1EMSRWT

Organum

4.   Watch this introduction to organum to see the basic difference between parallel organum, oblique organum, and florid organum.

    http://bit.ly/15ExwCz

Organum refers an early form of polyphonic music. The derivation of the term is obscure, but it may best be thought of as the consonant (pleasing) sounding of two notes simultaneously. Medieval musicians considered the consonant intervals to be the octave, perfect fourth, and perfect fifth. (The modern ear has a more expansive list of intervals it considers consonant.)

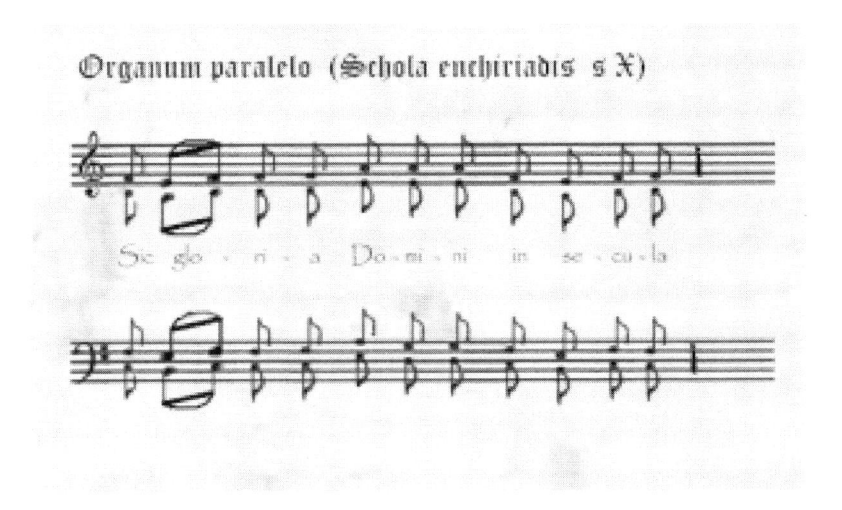

Example 1: Parallel Organum

Organum did not require the two voices to be always at consonant intervals, but consonance was a goal and thus a pervasive feature. One way to achieve consonance is to maintain the same consonant interval between the voices. This means the voices will move in the same direction to maintain that interval, resulting in parallel motion (Ex. 1).

Example 2: Oblique Organum

The original chant melody was called the *vox principalis* (principal voice) and the added melody (*vox organalis*).

Another form of organum could begin with oblique motion in which one voice stays at the same pitch while the other moves. This could be used in conjunction with parallel organum, allowing the singers to begin on the same note, use oblique motion as one voice rises to the consonant interval of a fourth or fifth, and then have the voices proceed with parallel motion (Ex. 2).

Once contrary motion between the voices was introduced, the style became much freer. In free organum, consonant intervals between the voices are predominant, but the interval is constantly changing.

Listening to Organum

5.   Listen to this example of free organum. You will see places where the organum is parallel and places where the voices move in oblique or contrary motion. In between are long single-voice melismatic passages that might be sung by the choir.

   http://bit.ly/1VT1Air

Organum takes on a more florid or decorative quality when the *vox principalis* is sung in long sustained notes while the *vox organalis* sings many notes. The voice singing the sustained notes of the chant is called the tenor. The Latin *tenere* means to hold (think "tenacity"). The chant serves as the ground on which the musical work is built. It is preexisting, fixed, and thus assigned the term *cantus firmus*.

In this short example by Leonin, you will hear the *cantus firmus* in long notes with an expressive, florid organal voice over it. Notice the free rhythm still being used.

   http://bit.ly/1uUHQm7

The introduction of rhythmic patterns, or modes, gives the chant a very new flavor. In Perotin's *Viderunt omnes* you will hear multiple voices singing florid melodic lines in rhythmic patterns while the *cantus firmus* (tenor) is drawn out to great lengths. Don't worry if all of these technical details aren't necessarily clear in your ear. Just focus on the *cantus firmus* as you listen. You may find a performance on YouTube, or look for a recording by the Hilliard Ensemble. You may find one here.

    http://bit.ly/1Bh5E0d

The full text is provided below.

Viderunt omnes fines terræ salutare Dei nostri. Jubilate Deo, omnis terra. Notum fecit Dominus salutare suum; ante conspectum gentium revelavit justitiam suam.	All the ends of the earth have seen the salvation of our God. Rejoice in the Lord, all lands. The Lord has made known his salvation; in the sight of the heathen he has revealed his righteousness.

Essay Question

Discuss the human tendency to make their music more elaborate. (You might make particular reference to performances you have heard of the National Anthem by various pop singers, or elaborations of some other musical work.) What advantages and what drawbacks (if any) are there to making such elaborations? How do they affect the way people perceive the music? Can you define certain limits on how far one should go in making music more elaborate?

42 Early Sacred Music – Assignments & Quizzes

Unit 9 Assignments

Key Terms (consult the Glossary)

A cappella
Autocephalous
Cherubic Hymn (Cherubikon)
Deacon's doors
Divine Liturgy
Filioque
Iconostasis
Kondakarion
Metropolitan

Old Believers
Orthodox
Otche Nash
Royal doors
Schism
Theotokos
Veneration
Znak
Znamenny

Key Names (consult the Who's Who)

Andrei Rublev
Kiril and Methodius
Tsar Alexei Romanov
Tsar Peter I (the Great)

Joseph Stalin
Sergei Rachmaninov
Tsar Ivan IV (the Terrible)

Key Places

Cathedral of Christ the Savior – Moscow
Cathedral of the Assumption – Yaroslavl
Church on Spilt Blood – St. Petersburg
Constantinople
Hagia Sophia
Kizhi
Moscow
Mount Athos
Novodevichy Convent – St. Petersburg
St. Basil's Cathedral – Moscow
St. Isaac's Cathedral – St. Petersburg
St. Nicholas Chathedral – St. Petersburg
St. Petersburg

Greek Chant

1.   Here, you can hear a sampling of Greek chant, with a richly enacted drone underneath the melody. It is being chanted by three Athonite (Mt. Athos) monks—only three!

　　　http://bit.ly/15MPTGp

Hagia Sophia

2.   You will find this brief article a useful introduction on Hagia Sophia which, after all, is the site where the Byzantine Liturgy developed and had its fullest expression (before 1453).

　　　http://bit.ly/1uUL7lk

Here is a second, not long, but extremely useful article that covers architecture and history, including the delicate, frustrating issues of restoration and provenance (to whom should this historically important church belong, who should be allowed to assist and oversee restoration, etc.). It may give rise to more of your own questions.

　　　http://bit.ly/1z3MLQ1

Hagia Sophia is also the subject of one of National Geographic's "Ancient Megastructures" documentaries. You can see an extensive preview of the program online. Look at www.natgeotv.com.

　　　http://bit.ly/1zlhqvx

The Iconostasis

3.   Look at this short article in the Orthodox pages of Wikipedia. It explains the Iconostasis well (and succinctly!), particularly the bottom tier, or row, of an iconostasis (which is what many parish churches will have, and nothing more).

　　　http://bit.ly/1yo5iTs

The photo below shows a rather simple Iconostasis.

Russian Orthodox Church, Xuan Che (CC BY 2.0)

The "Deacon's Doors" (north and south) can have different figures, but very common will be the icons of the Archangels Michael and George.

Notice the last two sentences of this article: "If there is a second tier, it will usually contain icons of the Twelve Great Feasts. Other tiers will depict the patriarchs, prophets and apostles." Click through to the link for the Great Feasts, and look at the tier of icons there. These are the twelve smaller icons that go directly above the first row.

QUESTIONS

    a.   How many of these Feasts are familiar to you?

    b.   Choose one that is not familiar and find out what it is all about.

Here is a link to find out what is included on the next row higher, known as Deesis.

    http://bit.ly/1EnTx7F

Realize the figures can be spread across a full row of the Iconostasis, or it can be a single icon with Christ, Holy Mary, St. John.

The row above the Deesis is devoted to the Patriarchs: the Old Testament Prophets, Kings.

4. Iconostases are not unknown in Catholic Churches, particularly when there is a strong mix of cultures. Here is an amazing one in a Greek Catholic Church in Hungary. Wouldn't you call that quite a mix of cultures?

Jojoje (CC BY-SA 3.0) http://bit.ly/1uw9lwC

Creating an Icon

5. In this video you will get to know an icon writer (painter) working in the United States. Primarily you'll get a very good sense of how he lives: the role of prayer and fasting, the simplicity of his life, relying on what we'd called pre-20th-century technologies. You'll hear strong statements about the spirituality necessary and gain a sense of his aesthetic values as well.

http://bit.ly/1BsXapd

Here in this video you'll see many details as to how an icon is written (painted), **including the technique of gold-leafing and egg-tempura.** (Adding the 18th-century music of Mozart as background music in this video is incongruous, however.)

    http://bit.ly/1H2ickz

Bell-Ringing

6.   Something once difficult to hear is now easily accessible on the internet. This video gives you a good view of both the bell ringer and the mechanism.

    http://bit.ly/1y0Xb04

Znamenny

7.   Start with this short clip. The choir's name is Glas vekov (Voice of the Ages). Here is their website. There will be commentary in this clip, between the singing, but the speakers' words are translated into English.

    http://bit.ly/1tirzq3

Don't be thrown by the brief second of "modern notation" you see around 3:40. They are, yes, singing off of modern notation. But that is not how this would have been notated.

In this clip, you'll hear *The Beatitudes* sung by two male voices, singing it within the concept of an actual service. You'll hear the priest chanting his text quickly at a slight distance from them. Note the contrast in style when the two singers of the choir enter with *znamenny* melodies. You'll hear the word *blazhenny* (blessed) sung many times.

Here is more Znamenny-style Orthodox singing, in English, from McKinney, Texas, very close to where I live.

    http://bit.ly/21KgXxt

In this clip, you'll hear *The Beatitudes* sung by two male voices, singing it within the concept of an actual service. You'll hear the priest chanting his text quickly at a slight distance from them. Note the contrast in style when the two singers of the choir enter with *znamenny* melodies. You'll hear the word *blazhenny* (blessed) sung many times.

> http://bit.ly/1VT32l4

Russian Romantic Choral Sound

8.   We cannot cover the full progression from the entry of Western musical influence, which changed *znamenny* by bringing in line-and-space notation, regular rhythmic patterns, Baroque, then Classical, and finally Romantic style to the choral singing of the Russian Orthodox Church. But it is important to make sure you have heard something of the full-blown Romantic sound of Russian Choral Music. For it is this sound that makes it so famous, particularly in the world of "Classical Music Lovers"—not all of the steps along the way. Often cited in this respect are works by Rachmaninov, such as his *All Night Vigil* (Vespers) or works by his contemporaries. These you can explore at leisure.

To illustrate this Romantic style in a shorter form, here is a famous, equally luscious 19th-century setting of *The Lord's Prayer* by Nikolai Kedrov. This is one of the most emblematic of Orthodox choral pieces.

> http://bit.ly/1uURjtD

Communist Destruction of the Churches

9.   The Soviets demolished many churches and converted many others to secular purposes. None was more prominent than the Cathedral of Christ the Savior in Moscow. Vladislav Mikosha filmed the demolition in 1931 as shown in this short documentary. Note that he lived long enough (1909-2004) to see the Cathedral rebuilt and reconsecrated in 2000.

> http://bit.ly/1JSnNWS

Here's another account of the Cathedral's history.

> http://bit.ly/18mteBP

Essay Question

Discuss some of the ways that music of Eastern Orthodox Christianity differs from that used in Western Christianity. What do you think would be the most significant difference(s)? What parallels can you draw between Orthodox music and Orthodox architecture and iconography?

Unit 10 Assignments

Key Terms (consult the Glossary)

Basilica
Cantiga
Chivalry
Codex
Courtly love
Didactic
Ecstatic
Goliards
Liturgical drama

Melismatic
Organum
Quem quaeritis
Relic
Rotunda
Shrine
Stoa
Tenere
Troubadour

Key Names (consult the Who's Who)

Alfonso X (the Wise)
Hildegard von Bingen
Lady Egeria
Pope Urban II
William IX, Duke of Aquitaine
St. James the Apostle

Constantine
Holy Elizabeth (Elizabeth of Hungary)
Pope Gregory VII
Richard the Lionheart
St. Bernard of Clairvaux

Key Places

Bingen, Germany
Church of the Holy Sepulcher
Constantinople
Limoges, France (Abbey of St. Martial)
Santiago de Compostela, Spain

Canterbury, England
Cluny, France
Jerusalem
Rome
Wartburg Castle

Caritas

The video opens with Hildegard von Bingen's *Caritas abundat*.

Caritas abundat in omnia, de imis excellentissima super sidera,	Loving tenderness abounds for all from the darkest to the most eminent one beyond the stars,
atque amantissima in omnia, quia summo Regi osculum pacis dedit.	Exquisitely loving all she bequeaths the kiss of peace upon the ultimate King.

Pilgrimages

1. The Metropolitan Museum of Art has a collection of essays and artworks pertaining to medieval pilgrimages.

    http://bit.ly/18mtLDQ

Read the primary essay and consider the following:

   a. How was architecture affected by pilgrimages? What purposes did architecture serve for the pilgrims?

   b. The essay talks about Paula being a disciple of St. Jerome. St. Jerome is perhaps best known for his work on the Vulgate. What is significant about this work and what is the derivation of its name?

   c. If you gone on a Medieval pilgrimage to Jerusalem, Rome, Santiago de Compostela, or Canterbury, what would you have expected to see and do?

2. Read about the Church of the Holy Sepulcher as it was originally constructed by Constantine and how it has changed over the centuries. (Notice that you can explore many other holy places at this web site.)

    http://bit.ly/1hkyg24

To get a different sense of what a pilgrim might have seen, you can do a virtual tour of various sites in and around Jerusalem at some different web sites, including the Church of the Holy Sepulcher and Church of the Nativity.

The Way to Saint James

3. The Way to Saint James has many materials concerning Medieval and modern-day pilgrimages, including information on the *Codex Calixtinus*. There are many other sites you can explore on the pilgrim roads to Santiago de Compostela in pictures and about the Cathedral.

    http://bit.ly/1EnUXzc

Here is a site that gives you a close look at the *Codex Calixtinus*. You can also find English translations online.

    http://bit.ly/1zlsc4Z

Lady Egeria

4.   Dr. Adams makes a reference in the video to Lady Egeria (alternatively Aetheria or Etheria). Her writings were translated into English by M. L. McClure and Charles Lett Feltoe as *The Pilgrimage of Etheria* (see Bibliography).

5.   The University of York has an extensive web site on Christian Pilgrimage that examines the phenomenon from both the religious and cultural perspectives. You may find many resources there to investigate this topic further.

http://bit.ly/1qxgil1

Crusades

6.   There are so many resources for studying the Crusades written from many points of view. The subject remains politically charged centuries later. These audio lectures are engaging and help explain the perspective of Christians of that time.

http://bit.ly/1CJeecs

Polyphony

7.   *Cunctipotens genitor Deus*, from *Codex Calixtinus*

http://bit.ly/1zR2Uew

The Organum at St. Martial of Limoges flourished in the 12th century. Listen to some examples and compare it to the rhythmic style of the Notre Dame School (Léonin and Pérotin) that flourishes at the end of the 12th century.

http://bit.ly/1EnVJMt

Troubadours

8.   Although this course is specifically about sacred music, we thought it would be useful to explore a few facets of secular music that help explain some of the musical directions of the time and some important developments on the horizon. Our brief discussion of the Troubadours in Aquitaine (including Limoges) and the related Minnesingers in Germany (and specifically the singers' wars at Wartburg Castle) may inspire you to look more closely at those styles.

Cantigas de Santa Maria

9.   The Oxford Cantigas de Santa Maria database provides a lot of information concerning the 420 Cantigas. *Quen a omagen da virgen*, sung in the video by the Ring Around Quartet, is No. 353. We have not found an English translation of the entire text, but the story is outlined here.

   http://bit.ly/1JwxCva

Essay Question

Identify a religious pilgrimage to you or someone in your family would like to make. If you have already undertaken such a pilgrimage, what was it, why was it chosen, and what was the experience like? How did (or might) music make this journey more meaningful or memorable?

Unit 11 Assignments

Key Terms (consult the Glossary)

Arch
Ars antiqua
Ars nova
Bellows
Buttress
Cantus firmus
Conductus
Fresco
Gargoyle
Gothic
Hydraulis
Ligature
Mensural

Motet
Organ
Organum
Pange lingua
Portative
Positive
Rhythmic mode
Romanesque
Stained glass
Summa Theologica
Trope
Vault
Vernacular

Key Names (consult the Who's Who)

Albert the Great
Franco of Cologne
Louis IX
Plato

Aristotle
Léonin
Pérotin
Thomas Aquinas

Key Places

Basilica of St. Denis
Chartres Cathedral
Limoges, France
Paris
Strasbourg Cathedral

Beauvais Cathedral
Cologne Cathedral
Notre Dame de Paris
St. Peter's Basilica
Ulm Minster

Pipe Organs

1.   The Ancient Greeks had invented an early version of the pipe organ, the *hydraulis*, before the birth of Christ, and yet we are beginning our discussion of the pipe organ late in this course.

List some of the reasons that pipe organs might not have been a significant factor in sacred music until the late Middle Ages.

List some of the reasons that pipe organs became so predominant in church music following the Middle Ages. Think about both aesthetics and technology, and perhaps some other considerations as well.

Refer to this site for a very brief overview of the history of the pipe organ:

> http://bit.ly/1TsXHCb

2. Depictions of St. Cecilia

Master of the Saint Bartholomew Altar (c. 1505-10)
St. Cecilia Playing the Organ (1501)

QUESTIONS

- a. St. Cecilia is pictured here with a small portative organ. Notice the bellows in her left hand. This image from the Saint Bartholomew Altarpiece dates from the early 1500s and shows an instrument similar to the one played in the course video.

- b. How does this peaceful depiction of St. Cecelia create a contrast with the actual facts of her life, particularly at its end?

c. What type of organ, if any, might St. Cecilia have actually encountered during her life in second-century Rome?

For some guidance on this question, read an encyclopedia entry for pipe organ technology and history. Here's one:

http://bit.ly/1Tsdv9x

Gothic Architecture

3. This video from 1986 gives a very straightforward and informative look at the architecture of gothic cathedrals as well as their construction and maintenance.

http://bit.ly/1z5Mb48

Also very informative (although in our opinion needlessly sensationalized) is this PBS production.

http://to.pbs.org/1mHKqoS

Agnus Dei

4. Listen to this chant version of the Agnus Dei.

http://bit.ly/1yL35WZ

Now listen to the short polyphonic setting of the Agnus Dei from the Tournai Mass (14th Century). The Tournai Mass is one of the earliest known polyphonic cycles of the Ordinary of the Mass. It slightly predates Machaut's Notre Dame Mass (to be discussed in the next unit). The style is straightforward and mostly syllabic except for two extended melismatic passages.

http://bit.ly/1zTvImx

Beata Viscera and The Worcester Fragments

5. *Beata Viscera*, performed by the Ring Around Quartet in this video for this unit, comes from the 13th-century Worcester Fragments.

The Latin text:

Beata viscera Mariae virginis,
Quae fructu gravida aeterni germinis
In vitae poculo propinat pro nobis
Et nostro vitio potum dulce dinis

An English translation:

Blessed is the womb of the Virgin Mary,
which, heavy with fruit of the everlasting seed,
carried with care the drink of sweetness
in the cup of life for mankind.

The Worcester Fragments are exactly that: fragments. Music historian Richard Taruskin comments in the Oxford History of Western Music:

> The wholesale destruction of "popish ditties"—manuscripts containing Latin church music—in the course of the Anglican reformation was a great disaster for music history. Between the eleventh century, the time of the staffless Winchester Tropers, and the beginning of the fifteenth, not a single source of English polyphonic music survives intact.
>
> All we have, for the most part, are individual leaves, or bits of leaves, that chanced to survive this medieval holocaust for a seemingly paradoxical reason: having become liturgically or stylistically obsolete, the books that contained them had already been destroyed. The surviving leaves had been recycled, as we would now put it, for lowly utilitarian purposes.

Listen to more from the Worcester Fragments in this extraordinary performance:

> http://bit.ly/1EourWn

Thomas Aquinas

6. Listen to the Eucharistic hymns mentioned in the video written by St. Thomas Aquinas.

Pange lingua

> http://bit.ly/1oSjZ42

Adoro Te Devote

http://bit.ly/1JzQYja

One can easily find numerous resources on Aquinas. A good place to start online would to search for the Thomas Aquinas Society. Students wishing to learn more about Aquinas might also start with the relatively short biography written by G. K. Chesterton with the unusual title *St. Thomas Aquinas. The Dumb Ox* (1933). And if you're not already a fan of Chesterton, you should become one.

Thomist philosophy has had its ups and downs over the centuries, its supporters and detractors. So where does it stand today? You might approach this question by looking at more modern Thomist philosophers. Although Aquinas did not write extensively on the subject of aesthetics, the 20th-Century Thomist philosopher Jacques Maritain deals extensively with that subject. We mention this in particular because our friend and contributor to this course John Trapani explains all of this in his book *Poetry, Beauty, and Contemplation: The Complete Aesthetics of Jacques Maritain* (Catholic Univ. of America Press, 2011). From the book's cover:

> Could it be that the world will be saved by beauty? Dostoevsky claimed as much. Aleksandr Solzhenitsyn thought so, too. But what is a Thomist to think? John Trapani, in his welcome study of Jacques Maritain's aesthetics, helps us come to terms with Dostoevsky's question.... –James G. Hanink, Professor of Philosophy, Loyola Marymount University

We confess our self-interest in promoting John's book, but the idea that the world can be saved by beauty is one we heartily endorse.

Dante

7.   *The Divine Comedy* is an epic poem widely considered to be the greatest work in the Italian language and also a landmark in Christian literature. It is beyond the scope of this course to study this work in detail. But we do want to consider the aesthetics of the time, and you should have some familiarity with the work. Read the following concise description:

http://bit.ly/27FJesM

Rod Dreher writes about Chartres Cathedral and *The Divine Comedy* as works whose beauty leads to the discovery of truth.

> The *Commedia*, then, is a work of unparalleled poetic beauty that teaches the reader that beauty prepares us for truth, and in turn, conforming our souls to that truth, we attain a measure of goodness, which makes it

possible for us to see more deeply into beauty, which reveals the nature of things. And so on, over and over, as we ascend to God.

Read the full Dreher article:

> http://bit.ly/21KipQk

QUESTIONS

- a. The article talks about beauty as a real thing as opposed to the Kantian notion that beauty is purely subjective. Do you subscribe to the oft-quoted idea that "beauty is in the eye of the beholder"? What arguments support your view?

- b. The article describes Dante's pilgrimage as an ascent from the finite to the infinite, from the appearance of beauty to Beauty itself. Does, or should, sacred music do the same thing? Is this the primary purpose of sacred music, or does it serve some other purpose in worship?

- c. Can you describe some particular kind of music, or characteristic of music, that would best draw the listener into an experience of beauty?

- d. What makes sacred music sacred?

Essay Question

Find points of comparison between the rise of Gothic architecture and the development of the more elaborate style of sacred music known as polyphony. Mention whatever you can about the historical chronology, advances in technology, and any other social, geographical, or cultural developments.

Unit 12 Assignments

Key Terms (consult the Glossary)

Ars antiqua
Ars nova
Ars subtilior
Black Death
Council of Trent
Danse Macabre
Divine Comedy
Great Famine
Hundred Years' War
Imperfect rhythm
Isorhythm
Italian ars nova

Ite missa est
Mass Ordinary
Medieval warm period
Mikveh
Perfect rhythm
Renaissance
Sanctus
Schism
Silk Road
Syncopation
Trecento

Key Names (consult the Who's Who)

Dante Alighieri
Franco of Cologne
Giovanni Boccaccio
Henry V of England
King John of Bohemia
Philippe de Vitry
Pope Clement VI

Francesco Landini
Giotto di Bondone
Guillaume Dufay
Joan of Arc
Petrarch
Pope Clement V
Pope John XXII

Key Places

Agincourt
Crécy
Rheims

Avignon
Notre Dame de Paris
Speyer

Ars Nova

1.   Guillaume de Machaut

We recommend listening to a complete performance of Machaut's Notre Dame Mass by Ensemble Gilles Binchois. It includes music from the Proper, not just the Ordinary composed by Machaut. It begins with the Introit *Gaudeamus omnes* followed by Machaut's Kyrie.

    http://bit.ly/1zdlhHM

2.   See this site for an overview of the major developments of the Ars nova. You will also find links to other relevant articles and resources.

   http://bit.ly/1K6avG4

Further Study on 14th-Century Turmoil

3.   Historian Ryan Reeves of Gordon-Conwell Seminary has a series of lectures on topics relevant to our study. His lecture on Medieval Society examines the three estates: church, nobility, and commoners and explains many of the changing dynamics of society from the early to late Middle Ages. You will also find a lecture on the Avignon Papacy that may assist in providing some context for the discussion in this last unit. You can find these and other lectures by Ryan Reeves at his YouTube site "Historical Theology for Everyone."

   http://bit.ly/1Di9l8g

4.   The BBC has a site explaining many facets of the Hundred Years' War. You can find quite a few materials, including video documentaries, on key events of the Hundred Years' War: the Battles of Crécy and Agincourt, and the life of Joan of Arc.

   http://bbc.in/1tt3Xz3

The Black Death in Art

5.   The Met Museum also has materials on the Black Death.

   http://bit.ly/1yOtTpb

The BBC examines the lasting impact of the plague.

   http://bbc.in/1CzXtQB

Speyer

6.   The town of Speyer, Germany sits on the Rhine River just south of Mannheim. We focused on Speyer's Jewish heritage, a very significant part of Speyer's history. In addition to the historic *mikveh* that we visited in the video, a new synagogue is being constructed next door. You can explore Speyer in greater detail at www.speyer.de.

While exploring the Speyer website, spend some time looking at Speyer Cathedral, the largest preserved Romanesque church in Europe.

Sanctus

7.   The Sanctus comes from Isaiah 6:3 and Revelation 4:8, and the Benedictus from Matthew 21:9.

   http://bit.ly/1Cgn6r9

We have covered to some extent each of the parts of the Ordinary of the Mass:

- Kyrie eleison
- Gloria
- Credo
- Sanctus (et Benedictus)
- Agnus Dei

If you belong to a liturgical tradition, you will have encountered these texts (and perhaps the chant settings) many times. You might also have encountered these texts within Christian traditions that are less liturgical or become familiar with them in other ways. Any serious study of music in Western culture requires familiarity with these texts and some understanding of their role within the Mass.

Dufay: *Ut quaent laxis*

8.   We have turned to this hymn on the Nativity of St. John the Baptist several times: first in our introduction to Gregorian Chant (Unit 1), in our discussion of early notation and the *solfege* of Guido d'Arezzo (Unit 8), and finally in the 15th-century setting of Guillaume Dufay. The original chant may have been unremarkable, but the accomplishments of Guido d'Arezzo and Dufay in setting it are praiseworthy. Listen again to the Dufay performance in video for this unit. You can find the work in modern notation at this link.

   http://bit.ly/1LiOSGa

Ut queant laxis resonare fibris mira gestorum famuli tuorum, solve polluti labiis reatum, sancte Joannes.	For thy spirit, holy John, to chasten Lips sin-polluted, fettered tongues to loosen; So by thy children might thy deeds of wonder Meetly be chanted.
Nuntius celso veniens Olympo,	Lo! a swift herald, from the skies

te patri magnum fore nasciturum, nomen, et vitae seriem gerendae, ordine promit.	descending, Bears to thy father promise of thy greatness; How he shall name thee, what thy future story, Duly revealing.
Ille promissi dubius superni per didit promptae modulos loquelae; sed reformasti genitus peremptae organa vocis.	Scarcely believing message so transcendent, Him for a season power of speech forsaketh, Till, at thy wondrous birth, again returneth Voice to the voiceless.
Ventris obstruso recubans cubili, senseras Regem thalamo manentem: hinc parens, nati, meritis, uterque, abdita pandit.	Thou, in thy mother's womb all darkly cradled, Knewest thy Monarch, biding in His chamber, Whence the two parents, through their children's merits, Mysteries uttered.
Laudibus cives celebrant superni te, Deus simplex pariterque trine; supplices ac nos veniam precamur: parce redemptis.	The heavenly citizens celebrate you with lauds, one God and at once triune; we also come imploring forgiveness; spare us among the redeemed.

Essay Question

Discuss the ways in which the development of more precise musical notation (described in the last unit of this course) changed sacred music, including the ways sacred music was created and performed. As you do this, you can draw on your understanding of styles of sacred music in later eras, including even modern styles of today.

Unit 1 Quiz

1. The term "monophonic" refers to
   a. music with a single note on each syllable.
   b. music with a single melodic line.
   c. music that is very quiet and relaxing.
   d. None of the above

2. In unmetered music, all of the notes receive the same accentuation.

   True / False

3. Reasons for singing sacred music include the following:
   a. To make it louder
   b. To make it more expressive
   c. To make it easier to memorize
   d. All of the above

4. Which of the following is not characteristic of Gregorian chant?
   a. Melodies are easy to sing.
   b. Musical rhythm is determined by the text.
   c. Melodies tend to move stepwise or to adjacent notes.
   d. It was intended to help worshippers engage in their own personal devotions.

5. Texture refers to the number of musical lines sounding simultaneously.

   True / False

6. Once we reach the time when musical manuscripts began to be created in the Middle Ages, we have all the information necessary to recreate the chant as it originally sounded.

   True / False

7. Pope Gregory's connection to the chant is
   a. a matter of legend.
   b. an historical fact.
   c. a recent discovery of musical researchers.
   d. a pure coincidence that they share the name Gregory.

8. For many centuries sacred music was taught and passed down by oral transmission.

   True / False

9. The earliest written musical manuscripts of Gregorian chant that we have discovered date back to the
   a. 2nd century
   b. 5th century
   c. 10th century
   d. 14th century

10. The aesthetics of chant require that it always be sung very quietly.
    True / False

Unit 2 Quiz

1. The Second Temple was originally built by King Herod the Great.

    True / False

2. The Western Wall of the Temple is significant to many worshippers because
    a. It is the only surviving part of the original Temple.
    b. It is the closest point to the Holy of Holies accessible to Jews.
    c. Muslim tradition says that it is the place of Mohammed's ascension into Heaven.
    d. None of the above.

3. The neighborhoods in the Old City of Jerusalem are divided into four sections or quarters:
    a. Muslim, Turkish, Christian, Jewish
    b. Jewish, Muslim, Armenian, Roman
    c. Christian, Jewish, Muslim, Armenian
    d. Greek, Christian, Muslim, Jewish

4. Psalm 137, which begins "By the Rivers of Babylon," describes
    a. The Jews being taken into exile by King Nebuchadnezzar.
    b. The destruction of the Second Temple.
    c. The Levites carrying the Ark of the Covenant across the Jordan.
    d. All of the above.

5. The term "apotropaic" was used in this unit to describe the ability of musical instruments to ward off evil.

    True / False

6. Musical research suggests that Jewish cantillation in the Second Temple bore little resemblance to the Gregorian Chant of the Middle Ages.

    True / False

7. Oral transmission is too unreliable to be considered a useful guide for reconstructing the music of past eras.

    True / False

8. The Dome of the Rock today sits on top of
    a. the site marked by Muslims as the place of Mohammed's ascension into Heaven.
    b. the site of the Holy of Holies.
    c. the site where tradition holds that Abraham almost sacrificed Isaac.
    d. All of the above.
    e. None of the above.

9. The shofar is one the oldest instruments known to mankind.

   True / False

10. Musical instruments played a significant role in the worship of the second Temple.

    True / False

11. "Antiphonal" refers to singing that is loud, harsh, and not refined.

    True / False

12. Synagogues were constructed to be houses of prayer for Jews who were not able to worship in the Temple.

    True / False

Unit 3 Quiz

1. The most important cultural center in the Mediterranean world in Jesus' time would have been
   a. Rome
   b. Carthage
   c. Athens
   d. Alexandria
   e. Jerusalem

2. St. Paul wrote his Epistles in which language:
   a. Greek
   b. Latin
   c. Hebrew
   d. Aramaic

3. The New Testament gives us some very detailed descriptions of music in the early Church.

   True / False

4. The Ancient Greeks understood music as divided into three types:
   a. Musica mundana, musica humana, musica instrumentalis
   b. Musica mundana, musica harmonia, musica instrumentalis
   c. Musica harmonia, musica humana, musica instrumentalis
   d. Musica mundana, musica harmonia, musica humana

5. Pythagorus is best known for writing on music from a perspective based in:
   a. Ethics
   b. Philosophy
   c. Mathematics
   d. Aethestics

6. The Ancient Greeks believed that music could be dangerous and might be harmful if not treated carefully.

   True / False

7. Which of the following did Plato put in a unique category because it is not perceived by the mind alone:
   a. Truth
   b. Beauty
   c. Goodness
   d. None of the above

8. Which is a stringed instrument generally associated with folk music?
    a. Aulos
    b. Kithara
    c. Lyre
    d. All of the above

9. Plato viewed music as an optional part of education – somewhat unimportant like competitive sports.

    True / False

10. A bell is an example of which type of instrument:
    a. membranophone
    b. aerophone
    c. cordophone
    d. idiophone

Unit 4 Quiz

1. There is not much surviving early Christian art because
    a. the early Christians were a persecuted sect with limited places to display art and limited resources to commission or pay for art.
    b. the early Christians, or many of them, may have believed art was forbidden by prohibition on creating graven images.
    c. Both A and B
    d. Neither A nor B.

2. Aniconic means having a negative view of icons or being opposed to icons.
    True / False

3. Christianity was legalized in the Roman Empire by
    a. the establishment of the Tetrarchy in 294.
    b. the Edict of Milan in 313.
    c. the Council of Nicaea in 325.
    d. the Edict of Theodosius in 380.

4. The period known as *Pax Romana* is generally dated from
    a. the establishment of the Roman Republic.
    b. Julius Caesar crossing the Rubicon.
    c. the rule of Caesar Augustus.
    d. the triumph of Titus in destroying Jerusalem.

5. The historian Josephus wrote detailed accounts concerning the destruction of the Second Temple.
    True / False

6. The term Liturgy refers to
    a. a fixed frame or series of texts used in worship.
    b. the part of early Christian worship that catechumens were allowed to attend.
    c. early Christian worship services conducted in the Greek language.
    d. None of the above

7. The early Church Fathers wrote primarily in which language:
    a. Latin
    b. Greek
    c. Hebrew
    d. Aramaic

8. Early Christians added elements to the traditional Jewish form of worship, including:
   a. The Eucharist
   b. The chanting of Psalms
   c. Scripture readings
   d. None of the above

9. Instruments were gradually discarded for use in early Christian worship because
   a. the early Christians did not want to use music similar to what was heard in the pagan Temples.
   b. the Romans authorities would not allow it.
   c. Plato had argued that instruments were dangerous and had a negative effect on people.
   d. the early Christians could not afford to hire instrumentalists.

10. The Eastern portion of the Roman Empire tended to be poorer and less culturally developed than the Western portion in Gaul and the Italian peninsula.

    True / False

11. Constantine fought a famous battle under the symbol Chi Rho at
    a. Actium
    b. The Rubicon
    c. Byzantium
    d. Milvian Bridge

12. Although St. Cecilia is generally considered the patron saint of music, that designation was originally given to St. John the Baptist.

    True / False

Unit 5 Quiz / Page 71

Unit 5 Quiz

1. St. Anthony lived for 20 years in the desert without seeing another human, after which he
    a. organized desert hermits into a community of monks.
    b. founded a monastery in Europe.
    c. became the Patriarch in Constantinople.
    d. continued his life as a hermit in the desert.

2. The biography of St. Anthony, influential in spreading the interest in monasticism, was written by
    a. St. Augustine
    b. St. Athanasius
    c. John Cassian
    d. John Chrysostom

3. St. Benedict established how many Daily Offices
    a. 5
    b. 6
    c. 7
    d. 8

4. Rome was sacked in which year
    a. 390
    b. 410
    c. 440
    d. 480

5. Monks in the early centuries of Christianity were frequently persecuted by the Romans.

    True / False

6. The office that occurs at noon is
    a. Sext
    b. None
    c. Vespers
    d. Lauds

7. The Rule of St. Benedict specifies
    a. when the monks should pray.
    b. how a monastery should be run.
    c. the specific types of discipline a monk must follow.
    d. All of the above

8. The Daily Offices are related to the morning and evening times for prayer in Synagogue services.

    True / False

9. Most of the text of the Daily Offices comes from
   a. the Psalms
   b. the Gospel
   c. Thessalonians
   d. Oral tradition

10. Compline is the last office of the day.

    True / False

Unit 6 Quiz

1. The Kyrie
    a. is a heartfelt cry for mercy at the beginning of the Mass.
    b. often has a musical style involving many notes on a single syllable of text.
    c. uses a Latin text from the Book of Isaiah.
    d. A and B, but not C
    e. A and C, but not B
    f. B and C, but not A

2. The Liturgy of the Word in the Mass retained many elements of Jewish Synagogue worship.

    True / False

3. The Eucharist includes which parts of the Ordinary of the Mass
    a. Sanctus and Credo
    b. Gloria and Agnus Dei
    c. Sanctus and Agnus Dei
    d. Gloria and Sanctus

4. The text of the Mass was written in a remarkably short period of time.

    True / False

5. The Church Year begins with
    a. Christmas
    b. Lent
    c. Easter
    d. Advent

6. Agnus Dei literally means
    a. Church Year
    b. Lamb of God
    c. Day of St. Agnes
    d. Bread of Life

7. The Mass may include the Eucharist, but it is not an essential element.

    True / False

8. Which of the following uses Greek rather than Latin text:
    a. Kyrie eleison
    b. Agnus Dei
    d. Credo
    e. Benedictus

9. Ornate melodies were excluded from the chant settings of the Mass.
   True / False

10. The term "catechumen" is applied to people who are:
    a. preparing for baptism.
    b. studying for the priesthood.
    c. full communing members of the church.
    d. worshipping underground to avoid persecution.

Unit 7 Quiz

1. Which two rivers historically formed an essential barrier between the Roman Empire and the northern Barbarian tribes?
    a. Danube and Rubicon
    b. Rubicon and Rhine
    c. Rhine and Volga
    d. Volga and Danube
    e. Rhine and Danube

2. Emperor Justinian I sent armies to Italy in an attempt to recapture parts of the former Western Empire.

    True / False

3. The dates of Mohammed's life [570-632] overlap the dates of which of the following:
    a. Charlemagne
    b. St. Benedict
    c. St. Augustine of Canterbury
    d. Clovis I

4. The Venerable Bede is remembered today primarily for
    a. efforts to convert the Germanic tribes.
    b. writings on English history.
    c. contributions to the development of musical notation.
    d. success in forging a strong alliance between Church and Crown.

5. The text of an antiphon always comes directly from scripture.

    True / False

6. Carolingian Miniscule represented an advance over previous methods of writing because
    a. it was faster to write and therefore allowed the copying of more books.
    b. it was smaller and took less space on the page.
    c. it was easier to read.
    d. All of the above

7. Charlemagne's desire to promote education was the result of his own rigorous training in the Liberal Arts.

    True / False

8. England was different from France and Spain in that most of its great Cathedrals were also monasteries.

    True / False

9. With the development of Neumes, it was finally possible to represent the musical pitches of a melody precisely.

    True / False

10. St. Augustine of Canterbury
    a. established a monastery in Kent
    b. established York as a center of learning
    c. was the first Archbishop of Canterbury
    d. a and b, but not c
    e. a and c, but not b
    f. b and c, but not a

Unit 8 Quiz

1. Manuscripts in the Carolingian era were mostly written on papyrus, which had replaced parchments a few centuries earlier.

    True / False

2. The most precious color for manuscript illuminations was:
    a. Gold
    b. Blue
    c. Red
    d. None of the above

3. The "provenance" of a manuscript refers to
    a. the symbols at the bottom of the page.
    b. the scribe who copied it.
    c. the original author.
    d. the places it has been.

4. Troping involved adding new words to an existing melody.

    True / False

5. Léonin and Pérotin were composers at the Cathedral of
    a. Winchester
    b. Notre Dame
    c. Milan
    d. Santiago de Compostela

6. Organum refers to the addition of which musical feature to the plainchant:
    a. Rhythm
    b. Additional melodic voices
    c. Instruments
    d. Long melismatic passages

7. The system of *solfege* (do, re, mi) is generally attributed to
    a. Paul the Deacon
    b. Charlemagne
    c. Guido of Arezzo
    d. Oscar the Hammer

8. Charlemagne lived a long life, especially considering the typical life spans of his time.

    True / False

9. *Ut queant laxis* is a hymn to
    a. St. Paul
    b. St. Benedict
    c. St. Athanasius
    d. St. John the Baptist

10. The typical scribe was given the job of copying a manuscript by rote, without making editorial or design decisions.

    True / False

Unit 9 Quiz

1. The City of Constantinople was conquered by Muslims in which year:
   a. 988
   b. 1054
   c. 1097
   d. 1453

2. Eastern Orthodoxy teaches the worship of icons.

   True / False

3. The word "orthodox" means
   a. right thinking.
   b. Eastern religion.
   c. bearer of truth.
   d. old belief.

4. "Autocephalous" refers to churches that are
   a. headed by an independent authority.
   b. governed by the local congregation.
   c. under the authority of the Pope.
   d. not under any authority.

5. Today, Hagia Sophia
   a. is a Christian church.
   b. is a Mosque.
   c. is a museum.
   d. has been torn down.

6. The *filioque* issue involves a doctrinal difference between Eastern and Western Christians regarding
   a. the Nicene Creed.
   b. the Rite of Marriage.
   c. the use of icons.
   d. the allowed depictions of the Virgin Mary.

7. Mount Athos is the spiritual home of Eastern Orthodoxy.

   True / False

8. The Orthodox church tends to be particularly fond of statuary.

   True / False

9. The Orthodox Divine Liturgy has little in common with the Western Mass.

   True / False

10. The Holy Trinity icon by Andrei Rublev
    a. depicts the Holy Spirit as a dove.
    b. depicts the three angels who visited Abraham and Sarah.
    c. depicts the vision of Isaiah.
    d. depicts three birds representing the three persons of the Trinity.

11. Bells in the Orthodox tradition do not play tunes.
    True / False

12. An Iconostasis is a wall that separates
    a. the altar from the rest of the church.
    b. the clergy from the worshippers.
    c. those baptized Orthodox from other worshippers and guests.
    d. All of the above

13. The music in Orthodox worship services remains primarily monophonic to this day.
    True / False

14. The Old Believers
    a. were encouraged by the communists to continue their traditions.
    b. died out long ago.
    c. are congregated around Mount Athos.
    d. continue to use only monophonic chant.

15. The Cherubikon is a hymn sung during the procession to the altar with the Bread and Wine.
    True / False

Unit 10 Quiz

1. The pilgrimage destination most important of all was
    a. Canterbury
    b. Constantinople
    c. Jerusalem
    d. Santiago de Compostela

2. Santiago de Compostela was built on the site where Saint James was martyred.
    True / False

3. Limoges was an important site for pilgrims on the their way to:
    a. Canterbury
    b. Constantinople
    c. Jerusalem
    d. Santiago de Compostela

4. The first Basilicas built by the Romans were intended for use as Christian churches.
    True / False

5. The Church of the Holy Sepulcher was built on the site identified by St. Helena as the site of the
    a. Ascension
    b. Crucifixion
    c. Resurrection
    d. a and b, but not c
    e. a and c, but not b
    f. b and c, but not a

6. "Quem queritis" was a popular text for plays performed in church on Easter.
    True / False

7. St. Martial organum was important for its development of metrical rhythm.
    True / False

8. Which of the following is true:
   a. Music carefully crafted by a learned composer tends to be categorized as ecstatic.
   b. The ecstatic and didactic clash at many points in Western music history.
   c. Didactic refers to music that lacks any emotional appeal.
   d. Vocal music is generally considered ecstatic whereas instrumental music is considered didactic.

9. The Goliards were wandering clerics who wrote secular songs in Latin.

   True / False

10. The concept of Courtly Love generally put women in a role subservient to men.

    True / False

11. The Miracle of the Roses is a story about
    a. Eleanor of Aquitaine
    b. Holy Elizabeth
    c. Hildegard of Bingen
    d. Joan of Arc

12. The Cantigas de Santa Maria are attributed to
    a. Alfonso the Wise
    b. Pope Calixtus II
    c. Richard the Lionheart
    d. William of Aquitaine

13. The "Peace of God" and "Truce of God" were outdoor events held by the clergy to attempt to convince the knights to cease their recklessly violent behavior.

    True / False

14. Polyphonic music became popular first and foremost in secular songs, and was only later brought into the church.

    True / False

Unit 11 Quiz

1. Dr. Chris Anderson cites two inventions as the most advanced feats of engineering: the pipe organ and what else?
    a. Flying buttress
    b. Harbor crane
    c. Mechanical clock
    d. Printing press

2. The Ancient Greeks invented an early version of the pipe organ that was powered by water.

    True / False

3. St. Thomas Aquinas is associated with which Greek philosopher?
    a. Aristotle
    b. Plato
    c. Pythagoras
    d. Socrates

4. Which three architectural advances enabled the building of gothic cathedrals.
    a. Pointed arch, treadwheel crane, flying buttress
    b. Ribbed vault, treadwheel crane, pointed arch
    c. Treadwheel crane, flying buttress, ribbed vault,
    d. Pointed arch, ribbed vault, flying buttress

5. Thomas Aquinas wrote the text for which of the following:
    a. *Adoro te devote*
    b. *Pange lingua*
    c. *Ubi Caritas*
    d. a and b, but not c
    e. a and c, but not b
    f. b and c, but not a

6. In the Mass, the Agnus Dei is sung immediately following the Kyrie.

    True / False

7. Franco of Cologne is important for writing a treatise, which:
    a. Explains a new system for notating rhythm.
    b. Explains a new system of rhythmic modes.
    c. Explains the requirements for the new Latin motet.
    d. Explains the use of organum in the St. Martial style.

8. People in religious paintings and stained glass could often be identified by the colors in which they were represented.

    True / False

9. In most of the gothic cathedrals, you will find the high altar on which end of the building.
   a. North
   b. South
   c. East
   d. West

10. Gargoyles were first created by architects building the gothic cathedrals.
    True / False

11. The gothic cathedral in this city was never finished, and today has no nave, after its roof collapsed during construction.
    a. Beauvais
    b. Cologne
    c. Rheims
    d. St. Denis

12. It was more difficult for medieval musicians to development a system for notating pitch than a system for notating rhythm.
    True / False

Unit 12 Quiz

1. Machaut's Notre Dame Mass includes a polyphonic setting of "Ite missa est," which is not part of the Mass Ordinary.

    True / False

2. Machaut was canon at which Cathedral?
    a. Chartres
    b. Notre Dame de Paris
    c. Rheims
    d. St. Denis

3. Imperfect rhythm occurs when the musical beat is subdivided into groups of 2 rather than 3.

    True / False

4. The name associated with 14th-century music "ars nova" comes from a writing of the time by:
    a. Franco of Cologne
    b. Guillaume de Machaut
    c. Philippe de Vitry
    d. Pope John XXII

5. The term "ars antiqua" is generally applied to the music of Léonin and Pérotin.

    True / False

6. Isorhythm is a compositional technique that
    a. involves rhythmic and pitch sequences of differing length.
    b. pits the tenor line against an upper voice.
    c. confines the music to just one rhythmic pattern.
    d. draws out the tenor line in long, sustained notes.

7. Syncopation occurs when the rhythmic stress is placed on weak beats.

    True / False

8. All of the Popes at Avignon (during the Avignon Papacy of c. 1305-1376) were
    a. antipopes in opposition to Rome.
    b. French.
    c. supporters of new music in the Church.
    d. opposed to the music of the French ars nova.

9. The Black Death devastated Europe's large cities but had far less impact in the countryside and remote villages.
	True / False

10. Ars subtilior
	a. literally means "subtle style."
	b. was a style characterized by extreme complexity of rhythm.
	c. was a style that quickly fell out of favor.
	d. All of the above
	e. None of the above

11. The Jews of Speyer were required to live on the outskirts of the city.
	True / False

12. Giotto was the architect responsible for
	a. the bell tower in the Florence Cathedral.
	b. the collapse of the Cathedral at Beauvais.
	c. the new St. Peter's Basilica.
	d. the Papal Palace at Avignon.

13. Machaut left a body of music that is predominantly sacred.
	True / False

14. The end of the Middle Ages would be marked by a desire to return to:
	a. Athenian democracy
	b. Biblical principles
	c. Classical ideals
	d. Thomist philosophy

Answer Key for Quizzes

Unit 1

1 b, 2 false, 3 d, 4 d, 5 true, 6 false, 7 a, 8 true, 9 c, 10 false

Unit 2

1 false, 2 b, 3 c, 4 a, 5 true, 6 false, 7 false, 8 d, 9 true, 10 true, 11 false, 12 true

Unit 3

1 d, 2 a, 3 false, 4 a, 5 c, 6 true, 7 b, 8 c, 9 false, 10 d

Unit 4

1 c, 2 true, 3 b, 4 c, 5 true, 6 a, 7 b, 8 a, 9 a, 10 false, 11 d, 12 true

Unit 5

1 d, 2 b, 3 d, 4 b, 5 false, 6 a, 7 d, 8 true, 9 a, 10 true

Unit 6

1 e, 2, true, 3 c, 4 false, 5 d, 6 b, 7 false, 8 a, 9 false, 10 a

Unit 7

1 e, 2 true, 3 c, 4 b, 5 false, 6 d, 7 false, 8 true, 9 false, 10 e

Unit 8

1 false, 2 b, 3 d, 4 true, 5 b, 6 b, 7 c, 8 true, 9 d, 10 false

Unit 9

1 d, 2 false, 3 c, 4 a, 5 c, 6 a, 7 true, 8 false, 9 false, 10 b, 11 true, 12 a, 13 false, 14 d, 15 true

Unit 10

1 c, 2 false, 3 d, 4 false, 5 f, 6 true, 7 false, 8 b, 9 true, 10 false, 11 b, 12 a, 13 true, 14 false

Unit 11

1 c, 2 true, 3 a, 4 d, 5 d, 6 false, 7 a, 8 true, 9 c, 10 false, 11 a, 12 false

Unit 12

1 true, 2 c, 3 true, 4 c, 5 true, 6 a, 7 true, 8 b, 9 false, 10 d, 11 false, 12 a, 13 false, 14 c